American City

American City

Detroit Architecture
1845–2005

Text by Robert Sharoff
Photographs by William Zbaren

A Painted Turtle book
Detroit, Michigan

Printed and bound in the United States of America by Meridian Printing, Rhode Island.
09 08 07 06 05   5 4 3 2 1

Library of Congress Cataloging-in-Publication Data

Sharoff, Robert.
     American city : Detroit architecture, 1845–2005 / text by Robert Sharoff ;
photographs by William Zbaren.
          p. cm. — (A painted turtle book)
     ISBN 0-8143-3270-6 (cloth : alk. paper)
     1. Architecture—Michigan—Detroit—19th century. 2. Architecture—Michigan—
     Detroit—20th century. 3. Detroit (Mich.)—Buildings, structures, etc. I. Zbaren,
     William. II. Title. III. Series.
NA735.D4S53 2005
720'.9774'34—dc22

2005018082

For Ella and Saima

Contents

Preface

In September of 2003, I drove to Detroit from Chicago with photographer William Zbaren to do a story on the renovation of the Book Cadillac Hotel on Washington Boulevard. The Book — at one time the city's most opulent hotel — was now a boarded-up hulk on a street that had definitely seen better days.

The scale of the building — it was the tallest hotel in the world when it opened in 1924 — was mind-boggling. That Detroit ever warranted a hotel of this size and magnificence seemed a little astounding.

Neither one of us knew much about downtown Detroit. Like many people, we derived our ideas about the city mainly from the often disturbing stories that appear from time to time in the national media.

Bill and I had a few hours between interviews and decided to take a walk around the downtown area. Detroit's central business district is oddly quiet at midday. Many of the enormous prewar office towers are either empty or marginally occupied.

And yet, everywhere we looked, there was a marvel of some kind: a flawless Beaux-Arts bank tucked away in the old financial district, half a dozen glittering Art Deco skyscrapers, a dramatic stainless steel fountain on the riverfront.

Back in Chicago, my curiosity aroused, I started looking for a book to explain downtown Detroit, to find out who designed what and how it all came to be. But with the exception of an excellent AIA guide by John Gallagher and Eric Hill, there didn't seem to be much available.

AIA Detroit, however, was a revelation. That Beaux-Arts bank? Stanford White. Those skyscrapers? Daniel Burnham, Albert Kahn, and a name I didn't recognize: Wirt Rowland. That fountain? Isamu Noguchi.

And there was more, much more, by some of the most formidable names in twentieth-century architecture: everyone from Cass Gilbert, Warren and Wetmore, and Paul Cret in the early days to modernists such as Frank Lloyd Wright, Mies van der Rohe, Minoru Yamasaki, and Philip Johnson.

Gradually, I came to realize the full extent of Detroit's architectural heritage as well as the favored position it once held among American cities.

I don't remember which one of us first suggested doing a book to document what we had just seen. But the idea, once it was out there, took on a life of its own.

The last large-format book on Detroit architecture was Hawkins Ferry's magisterial — but long out of print — *The Buildings of Detroit*, which was originally published in 1968. Since then, a number of buildings have been erected, and more than a few have been demolished. Certainly it was time to take a new look at a city that — through its principal industry — played a leading role in the development of modern American society.

An even more important consideration, however, was the sheer beauty of the structures we encountered. Detroit has some of the most impressive Beaux-Arts and Art Deco buildings and monuments in

Detail, Penobscot Building

the country. The modern period, too, is not without its glories. The fact that many of these structures are either endangered or marginally in use was a further spur.

Bill and I began in the summer of 2004 with a list of about ninety structures and — over the next nine months — gradually whittled it down to the fifty included here. Some were obvious choices — if there's one Frank Lloyd Wright building in town, then you photograph that building — but we had spirited debates about many of the others. The book is personal in that it very much represents our own feelings about what's good or great or interesting or necessary.

We had two guidelines: the first was to focus on commercial and civic buildings and monuments as opposed to churches and residences. The second was to show functioning buildings.

Then, having set these rules, we proceeded to bend them by including residential projects by two modern masters — the aforementioned Frank Lloyd Wright and Mies van der Rohe. We also decided to include the Michigan Central Railroad Station, a building too magnificent to ignore, even in its current ruined state.

As these photos reveal, there's another city hidden behind the frequently discouraging headlines.

Acknowledgments

This book could not have happened without the help and encouragement of many individuals. Three of the most important were Bob Wislow, chairman and chief executive officer of U.S. Equities Realty in Chicago; Kathryn Wildfong, acquisitions editor for Wayne State University Press in Detroit; and Peter Zeiler, business development coordinator of the Detroit Economic Growth Corporation.

On the basis of a handful of early scouting shots, Bob Wislow signed on to raise money to allow the book to be completed. U.S. Equities was one of the developers of the new Compuware Building in downtown Detroit, and Bob himself is an avid patron and fan of architecture.

On the basis of a single phone call from a total stranger (me), Kathryn Wildfong agreed to consider publishing what was then only a stray idea. And Peter Zeiler, a tireless promoter of the city, assisted us in numerous ways, large and small. Peter was instrumental in connecting us to the officials and executives we needed to deal with in order to coordinate a large, complicated project.

The book ultimately wound up being funded by grants from U.S. Equities Realty, Walbridge Aldinger Company, Compuware Corporation, and the Michigan Architectural Foundation. In addition, Sterling Group and SmithGroup provided office space in the Guardian Building, one of the city's premier landmarks, during the year we were in town photographing and researching the project. Many thanks to John Rakolta Jr., chairman and chief executive officer of Walbridge Aldinger Company; Peter Karmanos, chairman and chief executive officer of Compuware Corporation; Gary Torgow, president and chief executive officer of Sterling Group; and Carl Roehling, president and chief executive officer of SmithGroup.

We also received much-needed support and cooperation from a variety of landlords, managers, and officials. In no particular order, we would like to thank Steve Ogden, Danny Samson, and Lynnette Boyle of Sterling Group (Guardian Building); Doug Kuiper of Compuware Corporation; Matthew Cullen, Doug Rothwell, Conrad Schwartz, and John McDonald of General Motors Corporation (Renaissance Center); David Farbman of Farbman Group (Fisher Building and Wayne County Building); the Ilitch family and Greg Bellamy, respectively, owner and general manager of the Fox Theatre; Peter Van Dyke of the Detroit Institute of Arts; and Nancy Skowronski and Conrad Welsing of the Detroit Public Library.

Also: George Petkoski, owner of the Wright-Kay Building; Wendy Smith of Detroit International Bridge Co. (Michigan Central Railroad Station); Janae Stinson of the Detroit Police Department; Mary Beene of JPMorgan Chase; Linda Doolittle of HDC Partners, LLC (Buhl Building); Nick Tsalis, owner of the David Stott Building; Manuel Manrique, owner of the Turkel House; Robin Hines of AVI Foodsystems (McGregor Memorial Conference Center); Carmen Stiger and Delbert Greer of Habitat Company (Lafayette Park); Glen Blanton and Lynette Hill of Cobo Hall; John Kotcher of Grubb & Ellis (One Woodward); Jeff Boes and Jake Buehler of TMP Associates, Inc. (Cass Technical High School); Michael Boettcher of the East Dearborn Downtown Development Authority for information on the R. H. Traver Building; Karen Dumas, head of Detroit's Cultural Affairs Department; and Robin Boyle, associate dean of urban affairs at Wayne State University.

On the editorial side: many thanks to Steve Liska of Liska + Associates in Chicago, whose talent, enthusiasm, and unflappable demeanor made the project seem doable and even inevitable in the face of our periodic meltdowns; to Chris Newman, senior editor of *Chicago Magazine*, for her judicious editing of the photo captions; to photographer Tom Maday, for much-appreciated advice and equipment (and a fabulous author photo); to photographer Lindsay Gallup for answering the phone whenever we called and dispensing advice and encouragement in equal measure; and to Jane Hoehner, director of Wayne State University Press, for saying "yes."

Bill and I would also like to thank architect Eric Hill, co-author of *AIA Detroit*, who critiqued the manuscript and made numerous and important suggestions for improving it.

Thanks also to Ed Francis of Gunn Levine Architects and Carolyn Cardoza of SmithGroup for assisting us in various ways, ranging from room and board to contacts within the Detroit architecture community. Also, thanks to Margot Kessler, widow of one of Detroit's greatest modernists, the architect William Kessler, for providing information on her late husband.

Also, thanks to Sharon Burge, formerly of U.S. Equities, and Connie Dickinson of the Dickinson Group in Chicago for their early and much-appreciated support of the project. Also, thanks to Sheldon Broder for his advice on the business aspects of the project.

Finally, a round of applause for Rick, Christopher, Glenda, Gilbert, and the rest of the gang at the Guardian Building for making the whole experience a lot more enjoyable.

Grateful acknowledgment is made to the following, whose financial support has helped make *American City* possible:

PRINCIPAL BENEFACTORS

Compuware Corporation

Michigan Architectural Foundation

U.S. Equities Realty

Walbridge Aldinger Company

PATRONS

Leonard and Harriette Simons Endowed Family Fund

Dulcie and Norman Rosenfeld

Gwen and Richard Bowlby

Maggie and Bob Allesee

La Bonnie Bianchi Townsend

TMP Associates, Inc./Architects

IT PUBLIC L

HOUGHT INTO A COMMUNITY OF IDEAS OF THE WORLD
GE FOR HIS MIND'S NEW ADVENTURES AND THE UNDERSTA
HERE HE HAS HAD COMMUNION WITH THE SPIRITS OF O

AS WE KNOW LIFE IN OURSELVES WE WANT
TO UNDERSTAND LIFE IN THE UNIVERSE IN
ORDER TO ENTER INTO HARMONY WITH IT.

SCHWEITZER

Introduction

by Robert Sharoff

Detroit at its peak in the first half of the twentieth century was where the future was happening. The only comparison today would be to cities like Seattle or Palo Alto or even Hong Kong or Shanghai. "Come up to Detroit and see how we make things hum!" said a character in *Dodsworth*, Sinclair Lewis's 1929 novel set in the modern business world. A new invention as well as a new manufacturing process—respectively, the automobile and the assembly line—were being perfected here. Both had a profound effect on modern civilization.

Both also altered the city, transforming it from a regional manufacturing center to the industrial hub of North America, if not the world. New products and processes meant not only new buildings but also new kinds of buildings. Put simply, good design was good business. And good business, ultimately, translates to money. Detroit in the 1910s and 1920s was an extremely wealthy city. The result was the country's first high-tech metropolis.

It is tempting to equate the birth of Detroit with the automobile industry. The truth, however, is quite different. Detroit—in American terms—is a very old city.

The founder, Antoine de la Mothe Cadillac, was French, as were the fifty-some soldiers, farmers, and fur traders who arrived by canoe one morning in the summer of 1701. "The banks of the river are so many vast meadows where the freshness of . . . beautiful streams keeps the grass always green," he wrote. "These same meadows are fringed with long and broad avenues of fruit trees which have never felt the careful hand of the watchful gardener. . . . On both sides of this strait lie fine, open plains where the deer roam in graceful herds."

The city's first building, appropriately enough, was a church, Ste. Anne's. The parish, though not the building, still exists. It is the second oldest continuously operating Roman Catholic parish in the United States.

For the next sixty years, Detroit was a French city, as evidenced by the numerous French street names such as Beaubien, St. Antoine, Rivard, and Lafayette. Many of these streets represent the boundaries of what were called "ribbon farms." In order to give each farmer access to the river, land was subdivided into long strips—some as narrow as 200 feet—that began at the waterfront and extended back for miles.

In 1760 the British arrived after defeating the French in the French and Indian War. The population at that time—including those on the outlying ribbon farms—was about 2,000 residents. The British had a brief run in Detroit—thirty-six years—before being routed by General "Mad Anthony" Wayne in 1794. "The town itself," wrote Wayne, "is a crowded mass of frame or wooden buildings, generally from one to two and a half stories high, many of them well furnished, and inhabited by people of almost all nations. . . . The streets are so narrow as scarcely to admit carriages to pass each other."

On the morning of June 11, 1805, John Harvey, the town baker, knocked out his clay pipe on his boot and inadvertently set fire to a pile of straw, thus igniting a blaze that—within three hours—consumed the entire city. Surveying the destruction, Father Gabriel Richard, a priest at Ste. Anne's, murmured, "We hope for better things; it will arise from the ashes" (Speramus meliora; resurget cineribus). Years later, these words became the city's official motto.

Shortly afterward, Augustus Woodward, a federal judge who, as far as we know, had no training in either architecture or urban planning, proposed a new plan for the city. A friend of Thomas Jefferson's, he had lived in Washington, D.C., when it was being transformed under Pierre Charles L'Enfant's ambitious master plan. He envisioned something similar for Detroit. The plan—basically a series of interlocking hexagons at the heart of which were elaborate public squares, or "circuses," connected by broad boulevards—ultimately proved too rigid and impractical to be widely implemented.

Still, the portion of it that did get built—basically the downtown area from Grand Circus Park to the Detroit River—has a unique charm. Walk around downtown Detroit and the buildings seem to dance before you. Streets curve and angle in from all directions, and there is a profusion of oddly shaped blocks. Instead of a skyline of orderly façades, you see the front of one building next to the side of another next to the angled corner of yet another. The view is expansive and ever-changing.

 "Detroit will resolve into one of the greatest industrial islands on Earth," said E. B. Ward, a prominent industrialist and the city's richest man in the years after the Civil War. "With immense supplies of iron and copper to the north, coal to the south, the Detroit River in front and canals on either end, the city cannot miss."

He was right. The city took off in the latter half of the 1800s as a manufacturing center specializing in cooking stoves and ranges, shipbuilding, railroad cars and equipment, and drugs and pharmaceuticals. In 1864 the city's Eureka Iron and Steel Works produced the first commercial steel in the United States using the Bessemer process.

By necessity, the city's architects during this period were a versatile lot. Many functioned as builders and engineers in addition to being designers. Very few had any formal training.

"We have a number of most competent architects, thorough masters of their professions, having taste, good judgment, versatility and enthusiasm," wrote Alexander Chapoton, a builder who worked with many of the city's firms. "The forms of buildings in Detroit take on greater variety; there is less repetition of styles than in any other city. . . .

Drive about the streets of Detroit and you find the buildings have an individuality."

Stylistically, the city followed the prevailing national trends. The second half of the nineteenth century was a time of revivals: Gothic and Romanesque and numerous variations on French and Italian Renaissance styles that today are referred to as Neo-Classical or Beaux Arts. "Medieval relics furnish the required inspiration for all the best work of the present day," said George D. Mason of Mason and Rice, one of the city's most prominent architecture firms in the final decades of the nineteenth century. "In this country . . . we have had to come back from the log cabins and board shanties. We have had to draw upon the old country for everything. We are just beginning to have ideas of our own."

Two other architects were notable during this period: Gordon Lloyd and the family firm of Sheldon, Mortimer, and Fred Smith, respectively, father, son, and grandson.

Lloyd, an Englishman who had attended the Royal Academy in London, immigrated to Detroit in 1858. Over the course of a long career—he died in 1903—he designed numerous structures, everything from churches and residences to office buildings and theaters.

Sheldon Smith, on the other hand, is ultimately remembered more for the firm he created than for the buildings he designed. He arrived in Detroit in 1855 after spending a number of years in Sandusky, Ohio. He set up shop as Sheldon Smith, Architect, and enjoyed almost immediate success with a number of well-received civic commissions both in Detroit and around the state.

This was the beginning of the longest-running architectural dynasty in the city as well as what is now the oldest continuously operating architecture practice in the United States. Sheldon died in 1868 and was succeeded by

Mortimer. Fred took over after Mortimer's death in 1896 and, in 1907, reorganized the firm with two partners: Theodore Hinchman and designer Maxwell Grylls. The name at that point became Smith, Hinchman, and Grylls.

After Fred's death in 1941, the firm passed into non-family hands. Today, after several mergers, the name has been shortened to SmithGroup.

A letter from Mortimer to Fred written in the late 1870s gives a vivid description of what an average day was like for a busy Detroit architect: "They have brought in the chapel drawings I made for Wendell and want me to cheapen it $1,000 . . . tough job . . . things are getting along well with the Ferry building. Blay is putting the concrete down as they want it — no more trouble about that. They

Detail, Fisher Building

are hanging the chandeliers, first story, today. Don't like them very well, too light. Endicott [the tenant] had better to have consulted me, I think."

Overall, the picture that emerges of Detroit in the late 1800s is of a bustling regional manufacturing center not that different from Cleveland or Pittsburgh or other nearby cities and far from a global powerhouse.

 And then it happened. "The darn thing ran!" is how Henry Ford later described what happened early in the morning of June 4, 1896, when he cranked up his "quadricycle" — basically four bicycle wheels, a light chassis, and an engine — and took it for a spin down Grand River Avenue.

This is especially evident in the buildings designed by outside architects. In general, the firms that found the greatest acceptance here were from New York. The results were often impressive. Cass Gilbert's Detroit Public Library, for instance, is one of Detroit's finest structures, a lavishly detailed Renaissance palace set down somewhat improbably in a Midwest boomtown. Warren and Wetmore's Michigan Central Railroad Station compares favorably to the firm's earlier Grand Central terminal in New York.

The scale of the city changed dramatically during this period. Detroit went from being a regional trading post to a world-class industrial center very quickly. There wasn't time for succeeding generations of high-rises. The result is a lot of small buildings and a lot of tall buildings with not much in between. The overall look is Art Deco, but Art Deco in Detroit covers a lot of stylistic ground.

"We worked in the Greek, in the Roman, in the Romanesque, in the early Renaissance, late Renaissance," said Corrado Parducci, the city's leading architectural sculptor and ornament maker during this period. "Very little of the French, but we did do work in the English Revival of the seventeenth century, and also in the Adams, the later Georgian. And all these styles were at our fingertips. It was a unique experience."

Detroit may have imported easterners for certain high-prestige projects, but increasingly the bulk of the designing was done by local firms such as Albert Kahn, Inc., Smith, Hinchman, and Grylls, Donaldson and Meier, and Louis Kamper.

Two figures were especially important in this efflorescence of local talent: Albert Kahn and Wirt Rowland.

Kahn, whose family emigrated from Germany when he was boy, was an enigma in many ways. More or less self-educated, he designed a series of groundbreaking factory

From that point on, nothing was ever the same. Almost overnight, Detroit became the center of a world-transforming industry. During the boom years of 1900 to 1929, Detroit was home to dozens of automobile companies and literally hundreds of factories. These ranged from what we now call the Big Three — Ford, General Motors, and Chrysler — to brands such as Hudson, Chalmers, Packard, and Hupmobile.

During the same period, Detroit's population quintupled to more than 1.5 million residents, making it the nation's fourth largest city. In 1900, by contrast, it wasn't even in the top ten. The construction statistics are also staggering. For most of the 1910s and 1920s, there was more steel going up in downtown Detroit than anywhere outside of New York and Chicago.

For a number of reasons, Detroit tended to look east rather than west for architectural inspiration. The stripped-down Chicago school aesthetic appears to have had limited acceptance here. The result is that Detroit can be fairly described as the last eastern city rather than the first western one.

buildings—more than one hundred for Ford alone—that predated the International Style by several decades. His masterpiece was Ford's River Rouge Plant, an 1,100-acre site in suburban Dearborn that at the time it was completed in 1927 was the largest industrial complex in the world.

These projects, however, were only one part of his practice. He also designed numerous houses, churches, clubs, theaters, hotels, and office buildings in a variety of traditional styles. He had an encyclopedic mind and could do it all—modern factories, Tudor houses, Beaux-Arts office buildings. The idea that an architect should make a personal statement with a building probably never occurred to him. It was all about pleasing the client. "We architects may build in our own back yard anything as ugly and curious we please," he wrote. "But we have no right to do this for clients who rely on us to create that which will withstand the test of time."

This approach served him well. At the height of his career in the 1930s, he was responsible for 19 percent of all architect-designed industrial buildings in the United States. He was also active overseas, designing more than 500 factories in the Soviet Union alone. His enormous office—more than 600 associates at its peak—also served as a training ground for numerous other architects.

The other major figure in Detroit during this period was Wirt Rowland, a native of Clinton, Michigan, who worked for four different firms—including Kahn's—over the course of a forty-year career. He also, at the end, had his own firm, but by then the Depression had descended and commissions were few.

Rowland is something of a chimerical figure in Detroit architecture. For someone who survived well into the modern era—he died in 1946—there is a paucity of information on him. In part, this is due to his habit of working mainly for other people who were not necessarily eager or willing to share credit.

His unconventional personal life is another likely reason—he never married, lived in a rooming house, and spent long periods in Europe. Overlooked for years, he is only now being recognized for what he was: the city's leading skyscraper designer and the unseen hand behind a number of other important structures.

What is indisputable, however, is that during the 1920s in his role as chief designer for Smith, Hinchman, and Grylls, he created the three buildings that more than any others came to define downtown Detroit: the Buhl, Penobscot, and Guardian buildings. All three are astonishing in their mastery of form and scale as well as in the eclecticism of their ornament. The Buhl is medieval, the Penobscot a superb essay in Art Deco, while the Guardian combines Art Deco, Arts and Crafts, and Native American motifs in a style that defies easy classification. The Guardian is also notable for its riotous use of color, a radical departure then and now for office buildings.

Corrado Parducci supplied the ornament and remarkable relief sculptures for all three buildings. Parducci recalled lunching with Rowland while the architect "drew . . . his dreams on the tablecloth." Rowland "reached out, rather than looking back," he said. "He was a revolutionary in his ideas and effort."

The other major influence on architecture and design in Detroit in the early decades of the twentieth century was the Arts and Crafts movement. Arts and Crafts, which stresses individual craftsmanship, began in England in the mid-nineteenth century as a reaction to the Industrial Age. "The uniform machine-made products are made without pleasure and produce no pleasure," wrote William Morris, the movement's guiding theorist. "Factories are a hell wherein a man is hopelessly engaged in the performance of one never-ending and abhorrent task."

It is perhaps small wonder that Arts and Crafts found wide acceptance in Detroit, the most industrial city in America.

Detail, Detroit Receiving Hospital

modern structure that includes, among other glories, a Pewabic tile swimming pool.

No discussion of the Arts and Crafts scene in Detroit would be complete without mentioning Cranbrook, newspaper magnate George Booth's estate twenty miles north of the city that eventually morphed into one of the twentieth century's great design laboratories.

In 1925, Booth hired Finnish architect Eliel Saarinen—then a visiting professor at the University of Michigan in Ann Arbor—to assist in the design of a boy's primary school for the estate. It was the beginning of a landmark collaboration between the two men. Over the next twenty-five years, Saarinen designed numerous structures for Cranbrook, including an art academy, a museum, and a library. He also served as president of the academy as well as head of the architecture and urban planning department.

Saarinen's work embraced many of the features of the Arts and Crafts movement. His favorite material was brick, and he delighted in individual craftsmanship and handmade details. Still, his outlook was modern. "Our rooms, homes, buildings, towns and cities have become the innocent victims of miscellaneous styles, accumulated from the abundant remnants of earlier epochs," he wrote. "Our aims and ambitions have been lulled into servile acceptance of all this historic stuff, already obsolete for contemporary use long ago."

There are no Saarinen buildings within the city limits of Detroit. His ideas, however, proved extremely influential. Albert Kahn, for one, was highly impressed with Saarinen's submission to the Chicago Tribune's design competition for its new headquarters building in 1922. In a speech in 1937, he spoke of "a foreigner from Finland who had never built a skyscraper [who showed] us in his remarkable competitive design . . . the real solution of the problem."

The list of the artists associated with Cranbrook in the 1920s and 1930s—either

Art Deco, with its emphasis on streamlined design, reflects mechanical processes. Arts and Crafts does not. Still, in Detroit, the two achieved an interesting marriage. Many of the city's finest Art Deco skyscrapers feature handsome handmade details and ornamentation by a range of individual artisans and craftspeople.

A key figure in the local Arts and Crafts movement was ceramicist Mary Chase Perry, co-founder of Pewabic Pottery, Detroit's answer to Tiffany, Rookwood, Van Briggle, and the dozens of other local potteries that sprang up in this period. Pewabic, which Perry founded with Horace Caulkins in 1903, made everything from vividly colored ornamental tiles to vases and vessels of all sizes and descriptions. Known for its metallic and iridescent glazes, Pewabic ornamentation in the form of tiled mosaics, arches, entryways, and floors adorns numerous buildings in downtown Detroit.

Perry, a native of Michigan's Upper Peninsula, later married William B. Stratton, a talented architect known for his Arts and Crafts structures. Their great collaboration was the Women's City Club just north of Grand Circus Park, a strikingly as students, faculty, or artists in residence—is impressive. It includes designers Charles and Ray Eames, Florence Knoll, Harry Bertoia, and Ben Baldwin, architects Eero Saarinen (Eliel's son) and Harry Weese, and sculptors Carl Milles and Marshall Fredericks. (Fredericks went on to create *The Spirit of Detroit*, a large bronze sculpture that adorns the Coleman A. Young Municipal Center and also serves as the city's official symbol.)

 As in other cities, the fifteen-year gap caused by the Depression and World War II proved to be a decisive break with the architecture of the past. Very little was built during this period. The effect on many architecture firms was devastating. Smith, Hinchman, and Grylls, for instance, shrank from 250 associates to half a dozen.

But even these years had their glories. In 1932, Edsel Ford, Henry's son, commissioned Mexican artist Diego Rivera to create the *Detroit Industry Murals*. The murals—twenty-seven panels in all—occupy an entire room at the Detroit Institute of Arts, the old winter garden. The two main panels are an almost hallucinogenic rendering of life on the assembly line at Ford's River Rouge Plant, while the subsidiary panels depict a broad range of related activities, many in highly symbolic form. A panel depicting the origin of life and mankind's relationship to nature, for example, shows an infant curled up inside the bulb of a plant. Another panel shows what appears to be the baby Jesus being vaccinated by a team of doctors.

Rivera, a devout Marxist, was in awe of American skyscrapers and factories and the technology that made them possible. "In all the construction of man's past—pyramids, Roman roads and aqueducts, cathedrals and palaces—there is nothing equal to these," he said.

The murals caused a predictable fuss. George Booth's *Detroit News* called them "coarse in conception . . . foolishly vulgar . . . without

meaning for the . . . intelligent observer . . . a slander to Detroit workingmen . . . un-American." Other papers concurred, and numerous attacks by clergymen followed, along with calls for the murals to be destroyed. The museum ultimately held firm, and today the murals are widely regarded as the single greatest work of art in the city.

Detroit emerged from the Depression and World War II in relatively good shape. The automobile industry—which had switched to manufacturing war materiel during the conflict—went back to building cars for a country ever more enthralled with the idea of personal mobility. By 1950 the city was manufacturing half the world's automobiles.

In 1947 the city plan commission engaged the firm of Saarinen, Saarinen, and Associates to create a new plan for the mainly industrial riverfront. The plan they devised called for the creation of a civic center at the foot of Woodward Avenue consisting of a large public plaza framed on three sides by a new city hall and various other public buildings. It took thirty years, but much of this plan was subsequently enacted. The results ranged from satisfactory (Harley, Ellington, and Day's Coleman A. Young Municipal Center) to sublime (sculptor Isamu Noguchi's Horace E. Dodge and Son Memorial Fountain).

Architecturally, the postwar years were a time of big plans and experimentation with new styles and new technology. A new style—Modernism, or the International Style—was in ascendance across the country. The International Style stressed practicality and was well suited to the demands of large corporations. It found immediate acceptance in Detroit.

The architect who most successfully synthesized the city's taste during this period was Minoru Yamasaki, a second-generation Japanese American from Seattle who moved to Detroit in 1945 after being named chief designer of Smith, Hinchman, and Grylls. In 1949 he left and formed his own firm.

In an era when Modernism increasingly meant unadorned glass boxes—always a tough sell in Detroit—Yamasaki offered an interesting alternative. Although prototypically Modern in their lack of applied ornament, Yamasaki's buildings were beautiful in an almost old-fashioned way. He liked stone, he liked steel—the shinier the better—and he liked glass, especially when it gave him a chance to throw in a reflecting pool or a classically inspired statue or two. "I feel very strongly that man is much happier when his environment consists of delicate elements, beautifully proportioned, whether they are of wood or stone or concrete or steel," he wrote.

"Delicate" is an odd word to use in relation to Detroit, a city in love with big effects and broad strokes. And yet, Yamasaki's McGregor Memorial Conference Center, a white travertine structure on the campus of Wayne State University, may be the single greatest postwar building in the city. The goal, he wrote, "was to create a beautiful silhouette against the sky, a richness of texture and of form and a sense of peace and serenity." The results speak for themselves.

The city also continued to import some of the nation's top architectural talent for various projects. Both Frank Lloyd Wright and Mies van der Rohe completed commissions in Detroit in the late 1950s. Wright's project—a rare two-story Usonian house—is in Palmer Woods, one of the city's most exclusive residential neighborhoods. Mies's project was of a more imposing nature. The aim of Lafayette Park—a 120-acre residential development just east of downtown consisting of three high-rise apartment buildings and 186 town houses—was nothing less than the transformation and rebirth of the neighborhood in which it was located. The miracle is that it worked.

The 1960s and 1970s also saw the emergence of yet another remarkable local firm, William Kessler and Associates. Less idiosyncratic than

Yamasaki but consistently innovative in terms of form and color, Kessler provided the city with some of its best modern architecture. "It's fun to do something that never existed," he said. "That's the joy of architecture. Take something from thought and walk into it. Lives don't have to be lived as they were 100 years ago."

The firm was also a pioneer in a field that was almost nonexistent in Kahn and Rowland's day but became increasingly important in the latter decades of the twentieth century: the renovation and restoration of historic buildings. It's amusing to imagine what Kessler, a rigorous, Harvard-trained Modernist, must have thought of the excesses of the Fox Theatre, Detroit's most delirious 1920s movie palace. Still, the firm's 1988 restoration—executed under the direction of Kessler's partner, Ed Francis—is both intelligent and respectful.

 The postwar era came to a close with the construction of the Renaissance Center in the mid-1970s, one of the most ambitious urban renewal programs ever attempted in an American city. Detroit at that time was in turmoil from a variety of urban ills, among them racial unrest, depopulation, and economic decline. Into this breach stepped Henry Ford II, grandson of the man who—more than any other—was responsible for the transformation of Detroit over the previous century into the hub of a major global industry. Ford—along with a consortium of local business leaders—proposed an enormous new project on the riverfront in an effort to jumpstart downtown development. The architect was John Portman of Atlanta, at that time probably the most famous architect in the country.

"We had to do something that would stop the exodus from downtown Detroit," said Portman. "People and businesses were heading for the suburbs. To stop hemorrhaging of that magnitude, we had to prepare a design which would provide a major impact."

Detail, Guardian Building

He did and it did. Unfortunately, however, it wasn't enough. The city had been quietly losing jobs and residents for many years. This process accelerated in the 1970s and 1980s. From a peak of about 2 million residents in the late 1950s, the population declined to just over 1 million. During the same period, the total value of the city's property-tax base declined by two-thirds. Many downtown buildings were simply abandoned.

If there was an upside to the situation, it was that the decline resulted in the downtown remaining more or less intact at a time when other cities were losing historically significant structures on a pell-mell basis due to the rush of new development. The result is that today Detroit has one of the highest concentrations of excellent buildings from the late nineteenth and early twentieth centuries of any American city.

Things began to turn around in the early 1990s. In 1995, General Motors acquired the Renaissance Center as its new headquarters. It was a hopeful, if sobering, transaction.

A complex that cost $337 million to build twenty years earlier went for just $75 million. Since then, the company has completed an extensive renovation that includes constructing a dramatic glass winter garden on the south side of the complex.

Other positive signs for the downtown area include the construction of two new sports stadiums—one for football, one for baseball—as well as a major new office building in the heart of the central business district and an attractive new park.

Looking back, one sees a city that has continually reinvented itself through different eras and different economic circumstances. Detroit, in some sense, is where the modern American city took shape. (The fact that the world's first traffic light was installed here in 1920 alone guarantees the city some level of immortality.) But there's much more to the story, as the buildings so eloquently demonstrate.

American City

FORT WAYNE

6053 W. Jefferson Avenue
Lieutenant Montgomery C. Meigs
1845–50

In its early years, Detroit had many Federal-style structures, and this is one of the few remaining. Built to counter a British invasion that never materialized, Fort Wayne is both striking and a little beside the point. The imposing star-shaped ramparts — designed along lines laid down in the seventeenth century by French military engineer Sebastien Vauban — were obsolete by the time the fort was built. Still, the barracks building, with five symmetrical Federal-style stone bays, is impressively severe and monumental. Montgomery Meigs went on to have a long, illustrious career as a military officer and an engineer. In addition to serving as quartermaster general of the Union Army during the Civil War, he supervised the construction of the dome of the Capitol Building and chose the site for Arlington National Cemetery.

LIGHTHOUSE SUPPLY DEPOT

3766 Wight at Mt. Elliott Park
Major Orlando M. Poe
1874

Restoration by The Albert
Kahn Collaborative
1997

This solid, handsome public works project combines Romanesque and Italianate elements along with minimal ornamentation that probably had more to do with budget than aesthetic restraints. Orlando Poe's career—with one important exception— had a maritime cast. As chief engineer for the Upper Great Lakes Lighthouse District, he supervised the construction of numerous Great Lakes lighthouses and also designed and engineered the 800-foot Poe Lock at Sault St. Marie, then the largest ship's lock in the world. The exception was during the Civil War when—as chief engineer for General William T. Sherman during the latter's March to the Sea—he planned and supervised the burning of Atlanta.

R. H. TRAVER BUILDING

1211 Woodward Avenue
Gordon Lloyd
1889

By the time he died in 1904, Gordon Lloyd, then in his early seventies, was often referred to as the dean of Detroit architects. He made his name with a series of Gothic Revival churches in the 1850s and 1860s but later embraced a wide variety of stylistic influences, most notably Romanesque and Beaux Arts. Lloyd got better — or, at least, simpler — as he got older. The Romanesque Traver Building, a mid-block structure designed for a leading men's clothing firm and later occupied by the S. S. Kresge dime store chain, is notable for the delicacy of its ornament. The top-floor ballroom with its cast-iron columns and clerestory windows is one of the city's great — though unrestored — nineteenth-century interiors.

WRIGHT-KAY BUILDING (SCHWANKOVSKY TEMPLE OF MUSIC)

1500 Woodward Avenue
Gordon Lloyd
1891

With Wright-Kay, one sees Gordon Lloyd starting to come to terms with the modern office building. The structure is an interesting amalgam of old and new technology and styling. Traditional elements include a cast-iron frame, carved stone detailing, and a Queen Anne-style turret. But the building also incorporates newer ideas such as a bold, relatively unornamented façade and one of the first electric-powered elevators in the city. Designed for the F. J. Schwankovsky Company, a retailer of pianos, organs, and other musical instruments, it included a ground-floor showroom, a second-floor performance space, and offices above.

R. HIRT JR. CO. BUILDING

2468 Market Street
Architect unknown
1893

Merchant Rudolph Hirt Jr. constructed this Romanesque structure as a combination store and residence in the heart of Eastern Market, the city's old wholesale district. This is county seat architecture. One can imagine it across the square from the courthouse just about anywhere in the Midwest. The family continues to operate the store, which, over the years, has expanded into the top-floor residential apartment.

CHAUNCEY HURLBUT MEMORIAL GATE

**E. Jefferson Avenue at Cadillac Boulevard
(Waterworks Park)
Herman Brede and Gustave Mueller
1894**

Chauncey Hurlbut, longtime president of
the Board of Water Commissioners, left his
entire estate to the city to be used for the
beautification of Waterworks Park. The result
was this lyrical Beaux-Arts gate, which at
one time also contained a library. A bust of
Hurlbut once occupied the pedestal in the
center archway.

DETROIT CORNICE AND SLATE COMPANY

733 St. Antoine
Harry J. Rill
1897

Restoration and addition by William Kessler and Associates
1999

A cornice made of pressed and hammered sheet metal was commonplace in the
nineteenth century, but an entire façade was much less so. Harry Rill, known primarily
as a church architect, took his cues from his client, in this case a manufacturer of
pressed and hammered steel building ornament.

WAYNE COUNTY BUILDING (WAYNE COUNTY COURTHOUSE)

600 Randolph
John and Arthur Scott
1897

Restoration by Smith, Hinchman,
and Grylls and Quinn Evans
1987

Most major American cities at the turn of the century had a building or two like this one.
The style is Beaux Arts, the immediate inspiration the White City created for the 1893 World's
Columbian Exposition in Chicago, which launched the Classical revival in the United States.
The stately proportions and lavish interior mosaics and stonework make this one of the more
impressive examples of the genre. The building originally faced a similar structure—the old
City Hall Building, demolished in 1961—across Cadillac Square. Aside from this project, John
Scott is mainly remembered as the architect who gave Albert Kahn his first job and then fired
him a year later, claiming he had no aptitude for the work.

SAVOYARD CENTRE
(STATE SAVINGS BANK)

151 W. Fort Street and Shelby
McKim, Mead, and White
1900

Addition by Donaldson and Meier
1914

Nothing says more about Detroit's nascent
ambitions than the fact that one of its leading
banks contracted McKim, Mead, and White of
New York — at that time the most prestigious
architecture firm in the country — to design
its new headquarters. "It was the heyday
of conspicuous consumption," wrote
architectural historian Hawkins Ferry. "To
employ . . . McKim, Mead, and White as
architects was not only a guarantee of the
best in quality, but it was also the surest
route to social recognition." The firm's chief
designer, Stanford White, was at the apex of
his career as America's leading Classicist when
he designed his only Detroit building. It is
generally acknowledged that White was at his
best with smaller commissions, and with its
perfect proportions and restrained white
marble façade, Savoyard bears this out.

BELLE ISLE CONSERVATORY

Belle Isle
Albert Kahn
1904

Potted palms were an enduring obsession of the Gilded Age, especially when under glass. The models for this and numerous other conservatories of the period were England's Crystal Palace and the Palm House at Kew Gardens, both of which date from the mid-1800s. Albert Kahn, who spent a year in Europe sketching notable buildings at the beginning of his career, was undoubtedly familiar with these Victorian icons.

HARMONIE CENTRE
(BREITMEYER–TOBIN BUILDING)

1308 Broadway
Raseman and Fischer
1906

Renovation by Schervish Vogel Merz
1990s

At the turn of the century, the Harmonie
Park neighborhood on the northeast side
of downtown was the center of Detroit's
German community. The German-born
architect Richard Raseman did a number
of buildings in the area, including this
confident exercise in Beaux-Arts styling.
Originally built to house the offices of the
city's largest floral firm, it later became
home to a number of African American
professionals and organizations, including
the Brotherhood of Sleeping Car Porters.

719 Griswold Street
D. H. Burnham and Co.
1910

Renovation by Barton Malow Design
2001

"Uncle Dan was an impresario," said Frank Lloyd Wright, capturing the essence of Daniel Burnham's talent as well as the way he was regarded by fellow architects. In addition to orchestrating the 1893 World's Columbian Exposition and devising the 1909 Plan of Chicago — the first comprehensive plan for an American city — Burnham oversaw one of the largest architectural practices in the country. All of this left little room for designing, the bulk of which he delegated to a succession of talented associates. More than anything, Burnham was a synthesizer who specialized in combining the structural innovations of the Chicago school with the stylistic demands of Beaux-Arts Classicism. The Dime was the third of four D. H. Burnham and Co. commissions in Detroit. The first was the 1896 Majestic Building, now demolished. The second was the 1909 Ford Building, which stands a block south of the Dime on Griswold Street. The third, the David Whitney Building on the south side of Grand Circus Park, was completed three years after Burnham's death in 1912. The three remaining buildings are characteristic of Burnham's later work, which defined the modern office building in the early decades of the twentieth century.

L. B. KING AND COMPANY BUILDING

1274 Library Street
Rogers and MacFarlane
1911

L. B. King was a wholesale china company, and
it is probably no coincidence that the building
the firm commissioned for its headquarters
appears to be made of the same material. The
fanciful Italian Renaissance cornice was added
in 1926 and fits in surprisingly well with a
building that otherwise hews fairly closely to
early Chicago-style Modernism.

MICHIGAN CENTRAL RAILROAD STATION

Vernor and Michigan Avenue
Warren and Wetmore; Reed and Stern
1913

Designed by the same architects and engineers who created Grand Central Station in New York, Michigan Central is Detroit's most magnificent ruin, if not the country's. The building in its current state arouses powerful feelings of loss and regret, not uncommon emotions among preservationists in Detroit. Perhaps Richard Nickel, the late architectural photographer and preservationist, said it best: "Once we learn to appreciate what our architects give us, we will not be so prone to allow the destruction of our great buildings. Keeping them useful and maintaining them is a problem which will be solved in great part by our enlightenment in the spiritual realm, which is what life and architecture are all about."

R. H. FYFE'S SHOE STORE BUILDING

Woodward Avenue and Adams
Smith, Hinchman, and Grylls
1919

This fourteen-story terra-cotta skyscraper (the country's largest shoe store when it opened) is one of Detroit's most felicitous examples of the Gothic style.

ORCHESTRA HALL

3711 Woodward Avenue
C. Howard Crane
1919

Restoration by Quinn Evans and Richard Frank
1970–89

Known primarily as a designer of over-the-top vaudeville and movie houses (including the
Fox Theatres in Detroit, St. Louis, and Brooklyn), C. Howard Crane also did the occasional
legitimate venue. Orchestra Hall, the home of the Detroit Symphony Orchestra, was designed
and built in a hurry (six months from start to finish) to prevent the departure of an esteemed
conductor who was fed up with the orchestra's antiquated facilities. Elegant and subdued — with
superb acoustics — the building is an excellent example of Beaux Arts morphing into Art Deco.

DETROIT PUBLIC LIBRARY, MAIN BRANCH

**5201 Woodward Avenue
Cass Gilbert
1921**

**Addition by Cass Gilbert Jr. and
Francis J. Keally
1963**

"He chose forms, materials, colors, landscape, sculpture, and murals to compose visual symphonies," wrote the architect Hugh Hardy of Cass Gilbert, the designer of such landmark structures as the Woolworth Building in New York and the Supreme Court Building in Washington, D.C. Constructed over a seven-year period and at a cost of $2.7 million, the library was one of the most expensive civic projects in the city's history. In his proposal, Gilbert, a graduate of the École des Beaux-Arts, wrote that his aim was "a design which should be as pure and as fine an example of the best period of the Renaissance." The white marble building is, along with the Michigan Central Railroad Station, the city's most impressive Beaux-Arts structure. The central stairwell with its murals and elaborate ceiling is breathtaking. A later addition on the building's west side is respectful and occasionally brilliant on its own terms, as in the Saarinen-like crimson portico with its glass mosaics (see page xii) by the artist Millard Sheets.

CADILLAC PLACE (GENERAL MOTORS BUILDING)

3044 W. Grand Boulevard
Albert Kahn
1922

It is ironic that Albert Kahn, the "architect of Ford," created his two most enduring commercial structures—the General Motors Building and the Fisher Building across the street—for Ford rivals. Kahn's eternal fear of going too far—at least in his commercial commissions—is evident in the Classical detailing that was already a little passé by the early 1920s. Still, there is a wonderful delicacy to the beaded roofline as well as the first-floor colonnade. General Motors comprises four Burnham-style office blocks in a row. In terms of volume, it was the second-largest building in the world. The skill with which Kahn manipulated these huge forms testifies to an architect who knew how to think big.

WOMEN'S CITY CLUB

2110 Park Avenue
William B. Stratton
1924

Part Modern, part Arts and Crafts (William
B. Stratton was married to Mary Chase Perry,
the founder of Pewabic Pottery) with a hint
of Gothic in the deeply recessed windows,
this was an astoundingly modern building
for its time and place.

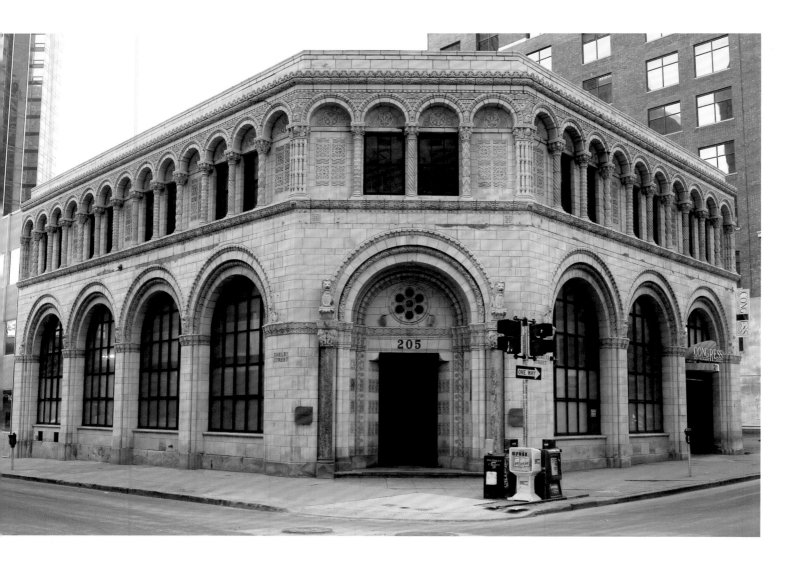

BANKERS TRUST COMPANY BUILDING

Congress and Shelby
Smith, Hinchman, and Grylls (Wirt Rowland)
1925

Less a building than a glorious façade, Bankers Trust, with its riotous Italian Romanesque ornament, appears to be the essence of Europe.

JAMES SCOTT FOUNTAIN

Belle Isle
Cass Gilbert
1925

Real estate speculator James Scott—a "vindictive, scurrilous misanthrope" according to one historian—guaranteed his own immortality by leaving $350,000 in his will for this fountain. "I have been unable to discover that there was anything inspiring about his life," said Cass Gilbert, who won the commission to design the memorial in a nationwide competition judged by, among others, landscape architect Frederick Law Olmsted. "But in this one act he has done more for the city than thousands."

BUHL BUILDING

535 Griswold Street
Smith, Hinchman, and Grylls (Wirt Rowland)
1925

The prevailing model for office buildings at the time, popularized by Daniel Burnham and others, called for interior light courts at the center of square- or U-shaped buildings. In his largest commission to date, Wirt Rowland reversed this formula with a cross-shaped building that freely combines Gothic and Romanesque elements. The results are mixed. On the plus side, every office has an outside window, and each floor has eight corner offices rather than the four in square-shaped buildings. The downside is that the building doesn't soar. There is a heaviness to it—reinforced by the medieval ornament—that seems at odds with the idea of skyscrapers. Still, the building is impressive. Rowland was nothing if not eclectic, and his version of Gothic includes two massive relief sculptures of Indian chiefs flanking the main entrance.

DETROIT INSTITUTE OF ARTS

5200 Woodward Avenue
Paul Cret
1927

Additions by, among others, Gunnar Birkerts and Harley, Ellington, and Day

"Nothing is more dreary than passing from a cream colored room with a coved ceiling and
inconspicuous door to another cream colored room with the same ceiling and the same door,"
wrote Paul Cret to the Detroit Arts Commission, the Detroit Institute of Arts governing board,
in response to a request for his ideas about design. The Institute is an odd blend of grandly
scaled Beaux-Arts public spaces and smaller galleries done in a variety of period styles and meant
to serve as backdrops for artwork reflective of those periods. The Beaux-Arts façade is enlivened
by an imposing entryway and also by reproductions of Michelangelo's *Slave* (see detail, p. xvi)
and Donatello's *St. George*. The Institute's most admired feature—though not by Cret, who
deplored what he considered the desecration of his building—is a series of murals by Diego
Rivera completed on the four walls of the building's winter garden in the 1930s. (A detail from
the murals is visible through the doorway depicted at left.)

FOX THEATRE

2111 Woodward Avenue
C. Howard Crain
1928

A newspaper reporter on hand for the opening of the Fox described it as "fashioned after the Hindoo Mosques of Old India, bewildering . . . in their richness and dazzling in their appointments." The Fox and other grandiose movie houses of the period were true people's palaces, meant to transport ordinary citizens to another realm where, presumably, the pressures of the outside world ceased to function. One sees the same impulse today at Disney World and in numerous Las Vegas hotel lobbies, and the recipe hasn't changed: bold colors, wildly eclectic references, and shoot-the-moon ornamentation. Beyond criticism and entirely gorgeous.

PENOBSCOT BUILDING

645 Griswold Street
Smith, Hinchman, and Grylls (Wirt Rowland)
1928

The second of Wirt Rowland's mighty trio of skyscrapers that redefined the city's skyline
in the 1920s, the Penobscot—at forty-seven stories—was the city's tallest building until the
construction of the Renaissance Center in 1977. The Penobscot was a departure for Rowland
after the Gothic-inspired Buhl Building down the street. Gone are the gargoyles, the randomly
sized terra-cotta blocks, and other medieval excrescences. In their place are the streamlined
forms and stylized ornament so characteristic of Art Deco. The building's power stems from
its size and massing, particularly the spectacular way Rowland handles the setbacks that form
the building's pinnacle. The minimal ornamentation is based on Native American motifs,
a perennial theme in downtown Detroit and one that Rowland would develop in a more
emphatic way in his final large commission, the Guardian Building.

PARK PLACE APARTMENTS (INDUSTRIAL BANK BUILDING)

232 W. Grand River Avenue
Louis Kamper
1928

Louis Kamper was one of the most prolific architects in Detroit and also one of the most problematic. A nineteenth-century Beaux-Arts Classicist at heart (he began his career working for Stanford White in New York), he never mastered the design of skyscrapers. The proportions are often off; the ornamentation, either banal or inappropriate. Midway through his long career — he died in 1953 at the age of ninety-two — he had the good fortune to meet the Book brothers, who were developing Washington Boulevard as a premier commercial district. Between 1917 and the onset of the Depression, he designed six major buildings for the street, including a seventy-story tower that was never erected. The Industrial Bank Building — a blend of Art Deco proportions and Beaux-Arts ornamentation that falls under the heading of High Gotham — is the best of the lot.

GUARDIAN BUILDING (UNION TRUST BUILDING)

500 Griswold Street
Smith, Hinchman, and Grylls (Wirt Rowland)
1929

Restoration by SmithGroup
2000

The Guardian represents the high-water mark of 1920s ebullience in Detroit with a floor plan resembling that of a medieval cathedral and a color palette like no other in the city. "We no longer live in a leisurely age," Wirt Rowland said at the time. "What we see we must see quickly in passing, and the impression must be immediate, strong, and complete. Color has this vital power." In the Guardian, color animates the marvelous detailing of the Pewabic tile semidome above the Griswold Street entryway, the riotous Rookwood barrel-vaulted lobby, and the red Numidian marble staircase leading to the vaulted banking room, with its elaborate mural and painted ceiling. The building is Rowland's masterpiece, as astounding in its way as the Chrysler Building, and one of the greatest Art Deco structures in the country.

DAVID STOTT BUILDING

1150 Griswold Street
Donaldson and Meier (John Donaldson)
1929

Architecture buffs in Detroit have long regretted that the Saarinens, Eliel and Eero, father and son, never designed a building for the city of Detroit despite being based for many years at Cranbrook in suburban Bloomfield Hills. But the Stott—an apparent homage to Eliel Saarinen's design for the 1922 Chicago Tribune headquarters competition—almost makes up for it. A slender, thirty-seven-story brick tower with a series of carefully graduated setbacks—and the best elevator doors in the city (see detail)—the Stott demonstrates that even at the end of his career, John Donaldson, a graduate of the École des Beaux-Arts in Paris, was one of the most skilled and versatile architects in Detroit. Donaldson also designed the St. Aloysius Church on Washington Boulevard and the seamless addition to Stanford White's Savoyard Centre on Fort Street.

FISHER BUILDING

3011 W. Grand Boulevard
Albert Kahn
1929

The first of what was originally projected to be three towers, the Fisher — commissioned
by the seven Fisher brothers of Fisher Body fame — is generally considered to be Albert
Kahn's finest non-industrial structure. The Fishers were intent on establishing a new business
district three miles north of downtown, across from the General Motors Building, and wanted,
according to Kahn, "a thoroughly high class building." They got one. The L-shaped structure
includes offices, a shopping arcade, and a 2,000-plus-seat theater. The overall effect is of an
almost unbelievable opulence. In the three-story, barrel-vaulted lobby are forty different kinds
of marble, enough, said one critic, to "dazzle the most jaded Roman emperor."

HORACE H. RACKHAM BUILDING

106 Farnsworth Street
Harley, Ellington, and Day (Clarence Day)
1941

This building, named for one of Henry Ford's original investors and occupied for many years by the Engineering Society of Detroit, is one of the few Art Moderne structures in the city. Art Moderne—also known as "stripped classicism"—was the final incarnation of Art Deco. The relief sculptures are by Marshall Fredericks, creator of the *Spirit of Detroit* sculpture that adorns the Coleman A. Young Municipal Center and also appears on the city's seal.

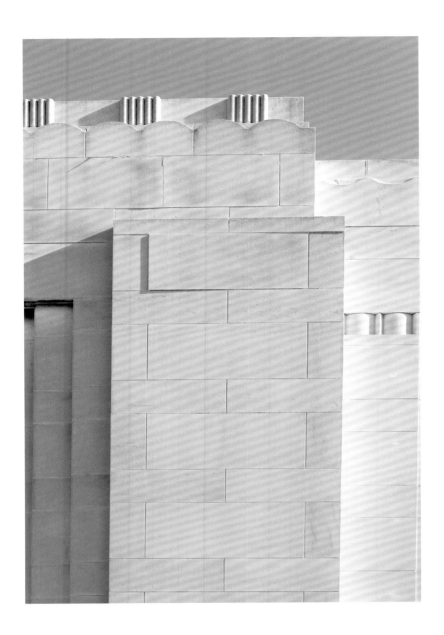

COLEMAN A. YOUNG MUNICIPAL CENTER (CITY COUNTY BUILDING)

Jefferson and Woodward Avenues
Harley, Ellington, and Day
1955

Crisply executed 1950s Modernism enlivened by the 1980s-vintage People Mover train. Marshall Fredericks's *Spirit of Detroit* sculpture is visible in the lower right-hand corner of the photo.

TURKEL HOUSE

2760 W. Seven Mile Road
Frank Lloyd Wright
1956

In a 1954 speech to the Detroit chapter of
the American Institute of Architects on the
subject of affordable housing for returning
GIs, Frank Lloyd Wright said, "I have given
it to him and he doesn't know it . . . in
what I call the Usonian Automatic." He also
explained how easy building a house can be
using "Usonian" techniques. "The GI can go
in his back road . . . he's got sand there . . .
get himself some steel rods and cement, make
the blocks and put the blocks together . . .
you can build your own house." The latter
is Wright at his most endearingly absurd.
This L-shaped, 4,000-square-foot house
is constructed of more than three dozen
different styles of concrete blocks, all custom
designed by the architect. Whatever else it
is, it's no do-it-your-selfer. The highlight is
a spectacular two-story, glass-walled living
room with built-in seating and bookcases
as well as one of Wright's trademark
open-hearth fireplaces. Among the quirky
details are nineteen exterior doors.

M^cGREGOR MEMORIAL CONFERENCE CENTER

495 Ferry Mall, Wayne State University
Minoru Yamasaki and Associates
1958

In a trip around the world in the late 1950s, Minoru Yamasaki, previously a strict Modernist in the style of Mies van der Rohe, found himself "strongly affected by the humanistic qualities of the historical buildings." Returning to Detroit, he resolved to strike out in a new direction, and his future buildings became more consciously expressive and idiosyncratic. The McGregor Memorial Conference Center is a masterpiece—a deceptively simple two-story white travertine structure divided into halves by a glass atrium. The building's exposed V-shaped ceiling beams affect other design elements, from the diamond-patterned atrium skylight to the dazzling aluminum doors. The structure is both dynamic and serene, a combination that Mies struggled to achieve. The landscaping, also by Yamasaki, features groves of trees and an exquisite water garden.

LAFAYETTE PARK

1 Lafayette Plaisance
Ludwig Mies van der Rohe and Ludwig Hilberseimer
1959–63

Ludwig Mies van der Rohe designed the buildings, Ludwig Hilberseimer oversaw the land plan. Lafayette is an anomaly—a 1960s-era urban renewal project that succeeded in renewing its blighted neighborhood. According to Franz Schulze, Mies's biographer, Lafayette is "closer than anything Mies ever designed to a realization of his ideas of modern architecture in service of modern American city living." The project—three high-rises and 186 town houses in a park-like setting—remains a top address in downtown Detroit. Along with the campus of the Illinois Institute of Technology in Chicago, Lafayette comprises one of the largest collection of Miesian "less is more" architecture in the world. The lush site was designed by the noted landscape architect Albert Caldwell.

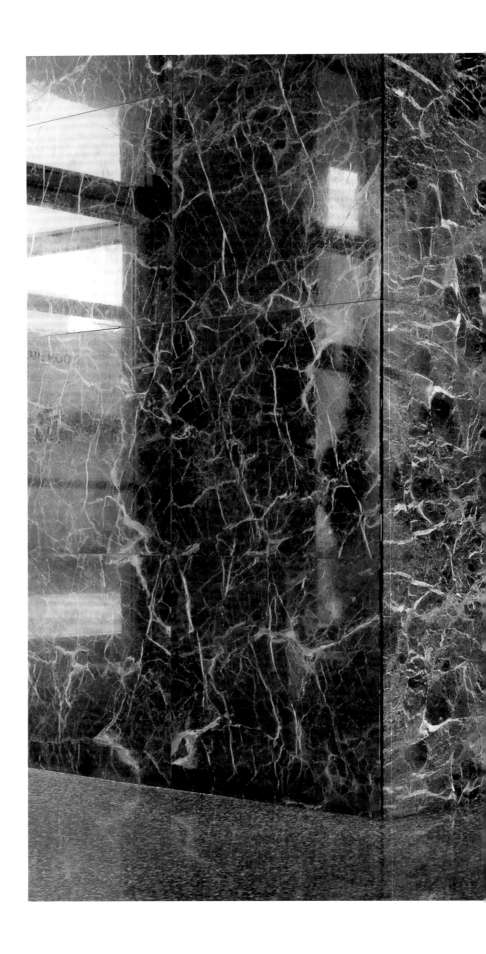

ONE WOODWARD (MICHIGAN CONSOLIDATED GAS COMPANY BUILDING)

1 Woodward Avenue
Minoru Yamasaki, and Smith, Hinchman, and Grylls
1963

One Woodward was Minoru Yamasaki's first high-rise and an apparent model for a later project, the World Trade Center in New York. According to Yamasaki, the distinctive narrow windows "offer magnificent views of the river and the city, yet they give a sense of security and relieve the feeling of acrophobia that many people experience in high-rise buildings." The three-story sheets of glass that enclose the white marble lobby were the largest in the world at the time.

FIRST FEDERAL BANK BUILDING

1001 Woodward Avenue
Smith, Hinchman, and Grylls
1965

This building — really two buildings connected by an elevator and utilities core — comes as close as any in Detroit to embodying modern corporate architecture in the 1960s. The one puzzle is how a straight-ahead Chicago-style steel and glass building came to be executed in charcoal gray granite.

FRANK MURPHY HALL OF JUSTICE

1441 St. Antoine
Eberle M. Smith and Associates
1968

The goal of Brutalism—a British architectural movement of the 1960s and 1970s that subsequently found wide acceptance in the United States—was to return Modernism to its roots. "No mystery, no romanticism, no obscurities about function and circulation" is the way one critic defined it. The Frank Murphy building fulfills this mission with a slablike concrete façade that clearly delineates the offices, court suites, and detention facilities of the building's interior.

SMITH, HINCHMAN, AND GRYLLS BUILDING

455 Fort Street
Smith, Hinchman, and Grylls
1910

Renovation by Smith, Hinchman, and Grylls
1970

This is a case of getting it right on the second try. Smith, Hinchman originally designed this rather ordinary building as a speculative office project, and over the years it was occupied by tenants. Then, in the early 1970s, the firm acquired the building to serve as its headquarters; an extensive renovation involved gutting the interior and installing an elegant glass façade that is held in place by what appear to be oversized aluminum jacks. This technology, new at the time, still looks amazingly contemporary.

KRESGE-FORD BUILDING

245 E. Kirby, College for Creative Studies
William Kessler and Associates
1975

Detroit's only Metabolist building. The
Japanese Metabolist architects of the 1960s
and 1970s believed that buildings should
have no beginning or end, that they should
be endlessly expandable in every direction.
Kessler, a Harvard-trained Modernist who
drew on a wide range of influences during
his long career, used this concept for a
building that manages to be simultaneously
modern, practical, and witty.

SBC BUILDING (MICHIGAN BELL TELEPHONE MAIN OFFICE BUILDING)

Michigan and Cass Avenues
Smith, Hinchman, and Grylls
1974

The building as folding screen with a front plaza featuring a sculpture by Alexander Calder.

RENAISSANCE CENTER

East Jefferson Avenue
John Portman and Associates
1977

Renovations by Skidmore,
Owings, and Merrill
2004

In the late 1960s and 1970s, John Portman
was one of the most famous architects in the
United States. The mixed-use projects he
designed for downtowns across the country
revived the idea of urban excitement and
glamour at a time when most large cities
were in decline. Portman's Brutalist complexes
usually combined office, hotel, and retail space
with enormous atriums. These vast spaces with
their raw concrete walls, bejeweled elevator
banks, shopping arcades, and revolving cafés
in water-filled lagoons set a new standard for
public amenities. The Renaissance Center was
conceived by industrialist Henry Ford II as an
urban renewal project following the 1967
race riots. There was a point to its formidable
appearance. "You've got to put something in
downtown Detroit that makes people want
to come," Portman said. In the late 1990s,
after General Motors acquired the 5.5
million-square-foot complex for its world
headquarters, the company undertook an
extensive renovation. Dropping a suspended
steel and glass walkway into the atrium
improved circulation; constructing an
enormous glass winter garden on the river
side of the complex provided light and
excellent views of the river.

HORACE E. DODGE AND SON MEMORIAL FOUNTAIN

Philip A. Hart Plaza
Jefferson and Woodward Avenues
Isamu Noguchi
1979

Isamu Noguchi described this fountain as an "engine for water," and so it is—a transcendent machine capable of producing everything from a fine mist to a drenching monsoon. Appropriately, the basin is shaped like a rain barrel.

DETROIT RECEIVING HOSPITAL

4201 St. Antoine
William Kessler and Associates, Zeidler
Partnership, and Giffels Associates
1979

William Kessler's work, says the architect
Eric Hill, has "the sleekness and finish of a jet
fighter," an apt description of this Modernist
complex clad in aluminum and porcelain. An
advocate of public art, Kessler chose the works
for the hospital's extensive collection.

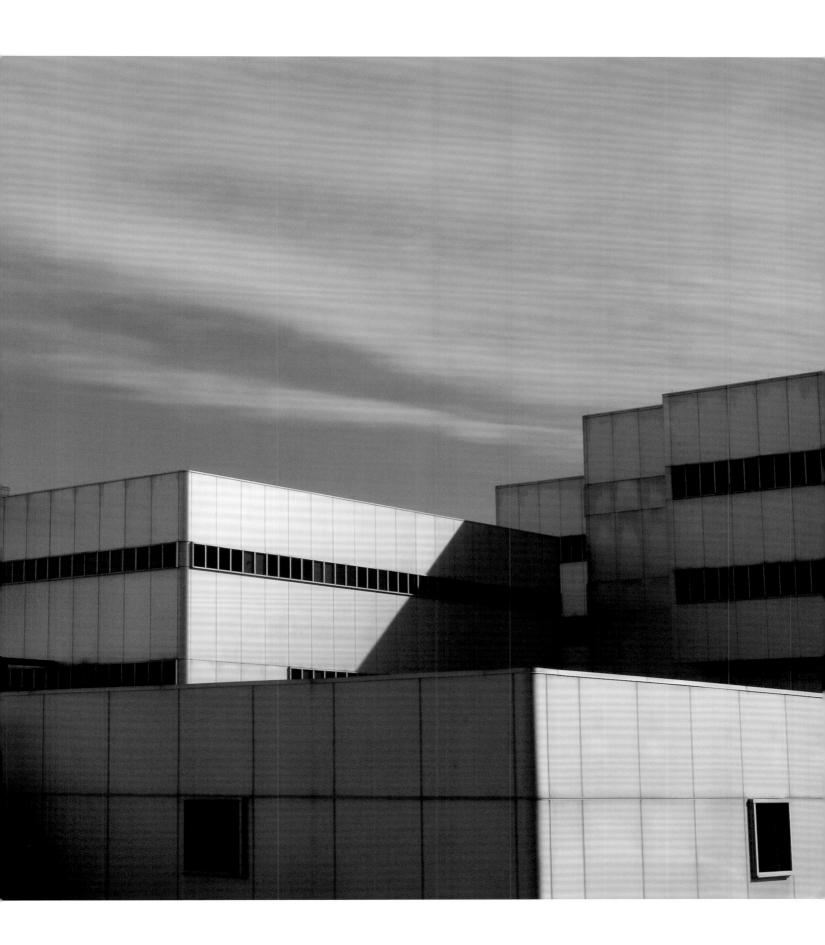

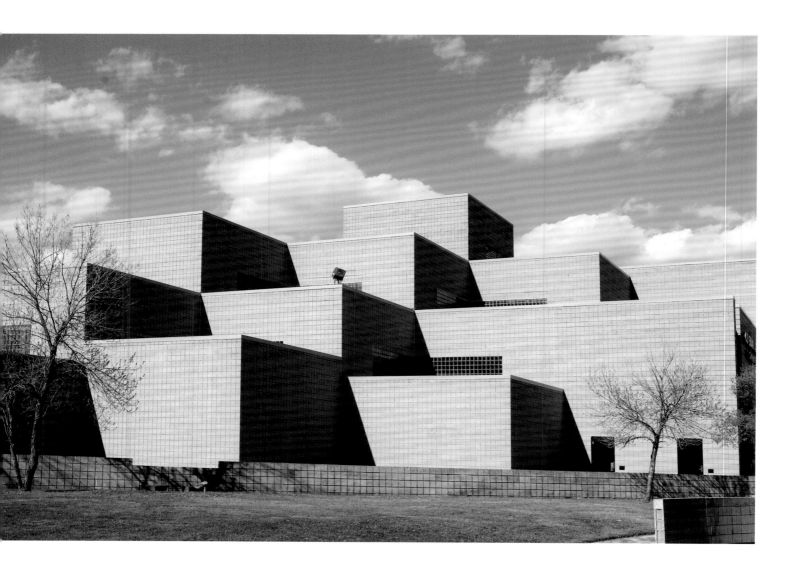

COLEMAN A. YOUNG COMMUNITY CENTER

2757 Robert Bradby Drive
William Kessler and Associates
1981

While officially attributed to William Kessler, this perfectly scaled Modernist pyramid is largely the work of the talented husband-and-wife team of chief designer James Cardoza and interior designer Carolyn Cardoza. The soaring two-story lobby with its bright green ceiling is a particular delight.

COBO HALL AND CONVENTION CENTER

1 Washington Boulevard
Giffels and Rossetti
1960

Addition by Sims-Varner
1989

The Rubik's cube façade—a product of the 1989 addition—is far more impressive than the building it adorns.

ONE DETROIT CENTER

Woodward Avenue and Larned
Johnson Burgee Architects
1992

Postmodernism got a late start in Detroit but soon moved into high gear with this Flemish-inspired building by Philip Johnson, the twentieth century's leading architectural gadfly.

JOHN D. DINGELL VA HOSPITAL AND MEDICAL CENTER

John R and Canfield
Smith, Hinchman, and Grylls
1996

In high Postmodern fashion, Smith, Hinchman, and Grylls humanized and enlivened this monolithic structure with multiple façades and one of the more unusual color palettes in the city.

CHARLES H. WRIGHT MUSEUM OF AFRICAN AMERICAN HISTORY

315 E. Warren Avenue
Sims-Varner
1998

The style, according to the architect Howard Varner, is "contemporary American" with "antecedents leading back to Africa." Representing the latter are the rope motif columns and the aluminum- and gold-plated masks above the main entrance.

COMPUWARE BUILDING

1 Campus Martius
Rossetti Associates
2003

The first major office building to be constructed downtown in a decade, Compuware Corporation's headquarters has already revitalized the area. The building's unusual footprint was determined by its site, a pentagon-shaped lot fronting Campus Martius, a prominent public square. The style is Modern, and sometimes aggressively so, as in the imposing glass entryway, but the tawny precast stone façade lends the building warmth and color. Like the Renaissance Center, everything revolves around the atrium, a stunning fifteen-story space containing a bamboo garden and the tallest "water attraction" in America.

CASS TECHNICAL HIGH SCHOOL

2501 Second Avenue
TMP Associates (Jeffrey P. Boes)
2005

An encouraging sign in Detroit today is that some of the best new buildings are schools. Cass Tech, a secondary school with a long history of academic and fine arts excellence, is the foremost example of this trend. An understated brick façade belies a sophisticated interior with enough high-tech flourishes to beguile even the most recalcitrant students. The materials—mainly brick and concrete blocks—are humble, the treatment anything but. The two-story cafeteria in the center of the building is a highlight, as is the top-floor media center. The latter is clearly indicated on the façade by a two-story metal grill.

Index of Buildings

Index of Architects, Architecture Firms, Designers, and Artists

Bibliography

Andrews, Wayne. *Architecture in Michigan.* Detroit: Wayne State University Press, 1967.

Brinkley, Douglas. *Wheels for the World.* New York: Viking, 2003.

Bucci, Federico. *Albert Kahn: Architect of Ford.* New York: Princeton Architectural Press, 2002.

Cahan, Richard. *They All Fall Down: Richard Nickel's Struggle to Save America's Architecture.* Washington, D.C.: The National Trust for Historic Preservation, 1994.

Chappell, Sally A. Kitt. *Architecture and Planning of Graham, Anderson, Probst, and White, 1912–1936: Transforming Tradition.* Chicago: University of Chicago Press, 1991.

Condit, Carl W. *The Chicago School of Architecture.* Chicago: University of Chicago Press, 1964.

Daskalakis, Georgia, Charles Waldheim, and Jason Young. *Stalking Detroit.* Barcelona: Actar, 2001.

Downs, Linda Bank. *Diego Rivera: The Detroit Industry Murals.* New York: W. W. Norton, 1999.

Ferry, W. Hawkins. *The Buildings of Detroit: A History.* Detroit: Wayne State University Press, 1968.

———. *The Legacy of Albert Kahn.* Detroit: Detroit Institute of Arts, 1970.

Gavrilovich, Peter, and Bill McGraw. *The Detroit Almanac.* Detroit: Detroit Free Press, 2000.

Grossman, Elizabeth Greenwell. *The Civic Architecture of Paul Cret.* Cambridge: Cambridge University Press, 1996.

Halberstam, David. *The Reckoning.* New York: William Morrow, 1986.

Heilbrun, Margaret. *Inventing the Skyline: The Architecture of Cass Gilbert.* New York: Columbia University Press, 2000.

Hill, Eric J., and John Gallagher. *AIA Detroit: The American Institute of Architects Guide to Detroit Architecture.* Detroit: Wayne State University Press, 2003.

Holleman, Thomas J., and James P. Gallagher. *Smith, Hinchman & Grylls: 125 Years of Architecture and Engineering, 1853–1978.* Detroit: Wayne State University Press, 1978.

Poremba, David Lee. *Detroit: A Motor City History.* Charleston, S.C.: Arcadia, 2001.

Portman, John, and Jonathan Barnett. *The Architect as Developer.* New York: McGraw-Hill, 1976.

Riani, Paolo, Paul Goldberger, and John Portman. *John Portman.* Milan: l'Arcaedizioni, 1990.

Saarinen, Eliel. *The Search for Form in Art and Architecture.* New York: Dover, 1985.

Schulze, Franz. *Mies Van Der Rohe: A Critical Biography.* Chicago: University of Chicago Press, 1985.

———. *Philip Johnson: Life and Work.* New York: Alfred A. Knopf, 1994.

Sergeant, John. *Frank Lloyd Wright's Usonian Houses.* New York: Watson-Guptill, 1984.

Waldheim, Charles. *Case: Hilberseimer / Mies Van Der Rohe Lafayette Park, Detroit.* New York: Prestel, 2004.

Woodford, Arthur M. *This Is Detroit, 1701–2001.* Detroit: Wayne State University Press, 2001.

Yamasaki, Minoru. *A Life in Architecture.* New York: John Weatherhill, 1979

In addition: The *Detroit News'* Rearview Mirror series; "Modern Man," Rebecca Powers, *Hour Detroit Magazine,* September 2001; the Burton Historical Collection at the Detroit Public Library Main Branch; and the Smithsonian Institution's Archives of American Art Oral History Interviews, Washington, D.C.